So Do I

Teacher's Choice Series

Elaine Moorefield
Colfax, North Carolina

Illustrations by
Steve Pileggi

⏺ Dominie Press, Inc.

The development of the *Teacher's Choice Series* was supported by the Reading Recovery project at California State University, San Bernardino. All authors' royalties from the sale of the *Teacher's Choice Series* will be used to support various Reading Recovery projects.

Publisher: Raymond Yuen
Series Editor: Stanley L. Swartz
Illustrator: Steve Pileggi
Cover Designer: Steve Morris
Page Design: Pamela S. Pettigrew

Published by:

ꝑ Dominie Press, Inc.

1949 Kellogg Avenue
Carlsbad, California 92008 USA

ISBN 1-56270-539-3

Printed in Singapore by PH Productions Pte Ltd.

3 4 5 6 IP 03 02 01 00

A fish likes to swim.
So do I.

A monkey likes to swing.
So do I.

A bird likes to sing.
So do I.

A frog likes to jump.
So do I.

A turtle likes to hide.
So do I.

A cat likes to take naps,
but I don't.